BRITAIN IN OLD PHOTOGRAPHS

WISBECH

ROGER   POWELL

&   ROBERT   BELL

SUTTON PUBLISHING LIMITED

Sutton Publishing Limited
Phoenix Mill · Thrupp · Stroud
Gloucestershire · GL5 2BU

First published 1997

Cover photographs: *front*: Hill Street bustling with traffic, *c.* 1910. Photo by C.W. Rutter; *back*: the First World War German U-boat engine recycled to generate electricity at the Wisbech Power Station in Sandyland, with workforce and families.

British Library Cataloguing in Publication Data
A catalogue record for this book is available from the British Library.

ISBN 0-7509-1279-0

Typeset in 10/12 Perpetua.
Typesetting and origination by
Sutton Publishing Limited.
Printed in Great Britain by
Ebenezer Baylis, Worcester.

CONTENTS

INTRODUCTION

Sometimes I play the game of '101 Facts about Wisbech', and although attention lapses before treble figures are reached the facts are not exhausted! The town was the birthplace of Thomas and John Clarkson, leading antislavery campaigners, of Octavia Hill, housing reformer and co-founder of the National Trust, and of the radical writer, William Godwin. Leverington may have provided the inspiration for Tony Lumpkin in *She Stoops to Conquer* and Emneth did provide that for *Toby the Tramway Engine*. Wisbech and Fenland Museum contains the manuscript of *Great Expectations* by Charles Dickens as well as that of one of the earliest Gothic novels, *The Monk* by Matthew Lewis (1796). The Museum itself is one of the oldest purpose-built museums in the country and dates from 1847. It was in Wisbech that possibly the first co-operative store was established and in 1720 one of the first workhouses was built. It is a small town packed with history.

The Romans came, saw and left their vestiges to be housed in the Museum! The earliest authentic reference to Wisbech comes from 1000, when Oswy and Leoflede gave the vill to the monastery of Ely when their son, Aelfwin, became a monk. In 1109 half the manor was given to the newly formed see of Ely. The etymology of the name derives either from the Anglo-Saxon for a stream or for a headland. In either case it is linked with the river Wissey or Ouse, which at this time joined the Nene at Wisbech and flowed into the Wash. Wisbech was the lowest bridging point, which probably accounts for its existence as a settlement. The Old Market was first so called in 1221!

Sometime in the later eleventh century the first castle was built, and during the Middle Ages the bishops of Ely developed it into an extensive site and the New Market developed outside its walls. The castle was one of the bishop's palaces and it made Wisbech an important administrative centre. In 1379 there is the earliest mention of the Guild of Holy Trinity and the bishops came to use this confraternity for much of the day-to-day running of the town. So when guilds were abolished in 1549, its officers became the first Capital Burgesses of the newly incorporated borough and their chantry priest became the first master of Wisbech Grammar school.

The bishops remained the lords of the manor, and in the 1580s the castle became a prison for Jesuits and other Roman Catholic priests. Perhaps it was here that the

Gunpowder Plot was first mooted! During the rule of Oliver Cromwell, however, all church lands were seized and the castle was bought by Secretary Thurloe who built a splendid mansion in the grounds. With the Restoration in 1660, the castle was returned to the bishop of Ely. The estate was bought in 1793 by Joseph Medworth for £2,305, but when he failed to reach an agreement with the Capital Burgesses for the sale of the mansion he demolished it, and in 1816 built the present Wisbech Castle, a smaller Regency villa. Around this he built two fine crescents forming an elegant Georgian circus.

The eighteenth and nineteenth centuries saw the height of the town's prosperity. In 1720 Bank House (known today as Peckover House) was built, and around it grew up the splendid Georgian frontages of the North Brink, which are reflected across the Nene by those of the South Brink, including the elegant eight-bayed house built for Sir Philip Vavasour in 1720 and in 1838 the birthplace of Octavia Hill. In the 1820s an impressive improvement programme of the Nene allowed Wisbech to become a thriving port freed from the threat of silting. One of those who made his fortune from the shipping trade, and who built the Victorian villa Osborne House, was Richard Young, but the leading family were the Peckovers. They were great benefactors to a range of institutions including the Museum and the Working Men's Institute.

The railway arrived in Wisbech in 1847 and, as there was no railway bridge over the river, a second line was built on the north side in 1866. With the development of soft fruit growing, the Great Eastern Railway Company built a steam tramway from Wisbech to Upwell, which took traffic from the canal that had opened in 1795. Now Wisbech has neither passenger railway nor canal.

In the twentieth century Wisbech has not expanded greatly and economically has come to rely heavily on food processing industries, although it is also an important printing centre and boasts its own two hundred year old independent brewery. In 1974 the town lost its borough status and became part of Fenland District, although it does still have a town council.

This book sets out to tell the story of Wisbech and area over the last one hundred and fifty years in photographs, for it was in Wisbech that an important photographic pioneer, Samuel Smith, worked. He realized how rapidly the town was changing so he used an instrument of the new technology to make a photographic record of the old before it gave way to the new. He also took a series of photographs for a report to parliament on the silting up of the Nene, the first time that photographs had been so used. Smith worked alongside another photographer, Thomas Craddock, who had his work displayed at the Great Exhibition in 1851 and bought by Prince Albert. This book publishes some of his work possibly for the first time.

When you take a photograph you appropriate the object photographed. You choose the subject and the aspect of it which you think the most suitable. We do not have a chance record but rather a selected one, and the degree of significance is chosen by the photographers. In a book like this that choice is further shaped by the compilers. We have chosen images which give a record of the past and the vanished, but we have also chosen images which are striking in themselves or have an individual aesthetic aspect. As photography became available to the general public, private memorials were created; now we are making some of these public and so turning them into shared images without the personal memories attached. We hope you will find these pictures of interest both as a historical record and in themselves.

We have divided the photographs into nine sections: 1. The Streets and Buildings of Wisbech, which offers a record of changes in the town scene; 2. Public Events, a photographic record showing Wisbechians in ceremonial and celebratory moods; 3. Fire and Flood, which reminds us of the two elements which most threaten the town; 4. Agriculture and Industry, which reflects the close relationship between these activities; 5. Shops, which shows some of the splendid emporia of old; 6. Education, which shows the town at thought and play; 7. Transport by rail, road and water; 8. The Villages, which presents images of the surrounding area – very much an integral part of the whole community.

Most of the photographs come from the very rich collection of the Wisbech and Fenland Museum, but I would also like to thank Anne and Nigel Elgood and Andrew Ingram for allowing the use of photographs from their personal collections. Finally and mostly I would like to thank Robert Bell, on whose encyclopaedic local knowledge the captions are largely based.

Roger Powell

Abraham Hooton, fishmonger, of 2 Little Church Street. Appropriately, the site of his shop is now a fish and chip shop. Reproduced from a lithographic slide of the 1890s.

STREETS
&
BUILDINGS

A splendid view of the Electric Theatre, Norfolk Street, c. 1920. Wisbech's first cinema was built by Mr T.H. Cooper in 1910. The theatre was later renamed the Regent before finally becoming the Onyx. In 1941 the cinema was hit by a bomb and had to be demolished. A car park now occupies the site.

A busy Edwardian scene along Church Terrace, *c.* 1910. The ladies on the right are gathered in front of Medcalf's blacksmith's premises.

This postcard, published by Bennett Bros of Wisbech in about 1915, shows a Victoria Road far removed from today's car-dominated thoroughfare. To the left is the Zion Baptist Chapel, built in 1856 and now used as a builder's store.

A postcard view of the Crescent taken from the tower of the parish church, with Medworth's villa in the right foreground, *c.* 1920. Joseph Medworth, a speculative builder, purchased what is known as Thurloe's Castle from the Bishop of Ely in 1793. Around twenty years later he razed the castle to the ground and built the present house and the Crescent. Later on, Medworth completed the circus with the laying out of Ely and Union Places.

The Rose & Crown Hotel and its predecessors have stood at the junction of High Street and Market Place since at least 1435 when the existence of the Swan is first recorded. The men in the foreground are sitting against the Jackson Memorial Fountain which was erected in 1879 by the Revd Henry Jackson, vicar of Wisbech St Mary, in memory of his father, the Revd Jeremiah Jackson, and his mother.

Preparations for market day in Wisbech Market Place just a few months before the outbreak of the First World War in 1914.

A detail from a *carte de visite* produced by Edward Johnson in about 1860, showing Wisbech Market Place looking towards Church Terrace. On the corner of Market Street can be seen the large grocery and drapery shop of Robert Wherry, four times Mayor of Wisbech.

This fine Georgian house, seen here in the 1850s, was acquired as an office by Richard Young, a local shipping magnate and five times Mayor of Wisbech. The house was demolished to make way for the present post office which opened in 1887.

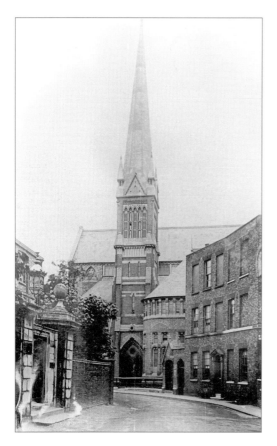

The Victorian gothic Baptist Church in Ely Place was designed by Mr H. Pooley, the Borough Surveyor, who lived around the corner in Museum Square. The church was completed in 1873 at a cost of around £5,000. The building was replaced by the neo-Georgian library which opened in 1975.

Norfolk Street, looking towards St Peter's Church, *c.* 1900. On the right is Heights Corner, named after the Height family who were originally stationers and booksellers here before running a sub-post office.

A broad and virtually traffic-free Lynn Road in the 1880s. Leach's Mill was one of the few eight-sailed windmills in this country; it was damaged during 'Windy Sunday' on 24 March 1895 when one of the sails was blown off and deposited in the Town Park. Two years later all the remaining sails were removed. St Augustine's Church, built in 1869, is on the right.

This postcard of Market Mews was published by Leach & Sons in 1927 and quaintly entitled 'Old Bit of Wisbech'. This was one of the many narrow lanes and passageways that at one time existed in the town close to the Market Place.

This lithographic slide of Marshland Row, the street linking Norfolk Street and Walsoken Bridge (later Coronation Bridge) was taken in the 1890s. One business that operated here at the time was Mrs Eliza Plater's tripe and cow-heel shop! Marshland Row is now called Norwich Street.

This postcard, from 'Kinsway Real Photo Series' published by W.H. Smith, shows Upper Hill Street before the First World War. On the left, the former Trinity Guild Hall and Grammar School are well covered with foliage. Further along is the Hippodrome Picture Palace. In the distance is Racey's Arcade, formerly Hill House, which was removed in the late 1920s and replaced by the Empire Theatre which opened on 22 November 1932.

Townshend Road, as depicted on a postcard published by Bennett Bros of Wisbech, *c.* 1920. The road was named after the Revd Chauncey Hare Townshend who bequeathed a magnificent collection of curios and *objets d'art* to the Wisbech Museum in 1868. Included in the Townshend Bequest was the original manuscript of *Great Expectations* by Charles Dickens. The manuscript can be viewed in the museum library on the first Saturday of every month.

A busy day in the Old Market, overlooked by the Victorian splendour of the Octagon Church, *c.* 1930. This was demolished in the 1950s and replaced by the Trustees Savings Bank. This postcard view was published by H. Coates.

Norwich Road, then part of New Walsoken, just before the First World War. In 1934 New Walsoken and parts of Old Walsoken were absorbed into the Borough of Wisbech. To the left is Walsoken Chapel of Ease. Built in the 1850s, the chapel was later occupied by the printing firm of Balding & Mansell. When this firm ceased trading in the early 1990s the chapel was demolished to make way for a housing development.

The people of Wisbech in their Sunday best assembling in Lower Hill Street at the turn of the century. Judging by the flags on display the town was celebrating a major event, perhaps the end of the Boer War or a royal coronation.

A fine prospect of Wisbech Market Place, *c.* 1915. This is another postcard from the W.H. Smith 'Kingsway Real Photo Series'. The passing of such splendid shops as W. Bray's cabinet & carpet warehouse, Selby & Son, and Dawbarn's is much lamented in this superstore age.

The South Brink, looking past the White Lion Temperance Hotel towards the Sessions House, *c.* 1915. The carriage was used to convey the hotel's guests to and from the nearby railway stations.

High Street, 1920s. Behind the men on the right is Brenner's Bazaar, the business that published the postcard from which this photograph is taken. The shop later moved to Market Place.

Messrs Wales & Wallace's surgery on the corner of Market Street, *c.* 1855. To the right is the shop of Thomas M. Pattrick, silversmith, jeweller and watchmaker. He also operated as a coal merchant from the same premises.

Bridge Street, 1885. The entrance to Peatling's wine cellars at the foot of the Clarkson Memorial can be clearly seen. To the right of the memorial is Lombard House, run by Alfred Loose, shortly before it was taken over by Evisons. This postcard view was published by Poulton's.

One of the few remaining seventeenth-century façades in the town, these houses in York Row may once have been owned by John Thurloe, Oliver Cromwell's Secretary of State. Over 150 years later they became the home of Thomas Clarkson, a leader of the movement to abolish slavery and the slave trade. The photograph was taken by Brown & Co., whose studios can just be seen on the extreme left, in about 1905.

Museum Square viewed from St Peter's graveyard, *c.* 1880. To the left is Castle Lodge which was constructed partly from material salvaged after the demolition of Thurloe's Castle. On the right is the Wisbech & Fenland Museum which was built to a design by Messrs Buckler of London in 1846/7. The cost, including the site, came to nearly £3,000.

Trevordale, Alexandra Road, *c.* 1920. This house was the home of F.J. Gardiner, the owner of the *Wisbech Advertiser* and author of the nineteenth-century *History of Wisbech*.

Albion Terrace, January 1947. Originally constructed as Wisbech's first purpose-built workhouse in 1720, it closed with the passing of the Poor Law Act of 1834 and the building of the new Union Workhouse off Lynn Road. The terrace, which was demolished in the early 1970s, stood not far from the present unemployment office.

The White Lion Commercial and Family Temperance Hotel photographed a few years before the present façade was built in 1883. The teetotal nature of the hotel was promoted by prominent local families such as the Peckovers. However, the premises are no longer dry.

The present town bridge, a fine neo-Georgian structure in concrete. At the time of its opening in February 1931, it was the largest portal bridge in the country with a span of 92½ feet. This postcard was produced by H. Coates & Son a few years after the bridge was opened.

This is the temporary wooden bridge that was used during the demolition of the Old Stone Bridge and the construction of the Iron Bridge, 1855–7; it was photographed by Samuel Smith.

Lawson's granary on the South Brink, probably photographed by Thomas Craddock, *c.* 1850. This, along with many other buildings in the vicinity, was demolished a few years later to make way for the building of the Iron Bridge.

In the days before mechanization the best way to keep the grass in the Town Park to an acceptable length was to use sheep. Accordingly, the Corporation regularly let the grazing rights in the park to local farmers – this also provided some extra revenue for the council. This explains the pastoral scene captured by H. Coates & Son between the wars.

Originally called the Robin Hood, this pub was renamed the Friendship Inn in 1897. It was situated at the corner of Little Church Street and the passageway which leads to Market Place. It is shown here in the 1950s. (*Courtesy of Elgood & Sons*)

Situated in Bridge Street, the Spread Eagle was at one time called the Eagle Tavern. This view of the pub was taken sometime before the building was refronted in 1932. (*Courtesy of Elgood & Sons*)

St Peter's Church viewed from the south-west, *c.* 1900. To the right is the south porch, once the home of the town library formed by the Corporation in the seventeenth century. The porch may also have been the first schoolroom for the Grammar School.

Exley's counting house, the single-storeyed building next to the King's Head, *c.* 1860. This property made way for Gurney & Co.'s new bank (of which the Peckover family were partners), which opened in 1879 and is now Barclays Bank's main branch in Wisbech.

Church Terrace in the 1950s, photographed by H. Coates & Son. The freshly laid out St Peter's Gardens can be seen on the left, while to the right the terrace is dominated by the Methodist Chapel which was replaced in 1969 by the present Trinity Methodist Church.

The Union Workhouse off Lynn Road, photographed by Samuel Smith on 20 September 1853. This imposing building was constructed under the Poor Law Act of 1834 which formed the Wisbech Union; it replaced the eighteenth-century workhouse on Albion Terrace, as well as several smaller workhouses which had been maintained by individual parishes in the district. Later it was known as the Clarkson Hospital, and was demolished in 1982.

The library in Peckover House, 1890s. The valuable collection of books was removed on the death of the Hon. Alexandrine Peckover in 1948 when the house was bequeathed to the National Trust. It is hoped to restore the library to its former glory.

PUBLIC EVENTS

The opening of the concrete bridge on Wednesday 4 February 1931. In the leading car, driven by Leslie Humphrey, were J.E. Sandall, Mayor of Wisbech, and Alderman H.A. Whittome, Chairman of the Highways and Bridges Committee, who had jointly opened the bridge.

Laying the foundation stone at the new Hill Street Baptist Sunday School, 20 April 1910. The stones were laid by Mr MacAlpine (who was presented with a silver trowel), J. Cockett (Hon. Pastor), Mr Gardiner (Deacon) and J. Tyers (Sunday School teacher and superintendent). This postcard was produced by Brown & Co.

A crowded High Street on Statute Day, *c.* 1911.

Miss Anna Jane Peckover and members of the Salvation Army pose for J.L. Brown, of the Borough Studio, behind a superb display of produce for Harvest Festival, *c.* 1910.

This view from a lithographic slide shows the funeral procession of David Pope, acting clerk and verger of Wisbech St Peter's Church, moving along Church Terrace. Pope was buried in the cemetery off King's Walk on 15 February 1911.

Walsoken Primitive Methodist Sunday School outing, *c.* 1914. On the right is John W. Wing, the superintendent. This postcard was published by C.W. Rutter.

Celebration of the Golden Jubilee of the Salvation Army, held at Ely Place Baptist Church, 1919. On the right are Miss Anna Jane and Miss Alexandrine Peckover.

Miss Anna Jane Peckover with visiting
Salvationists on the steps of Bank House,
20 October 1924. On her left are Mrs
Bramwell Booth, Miss Olive Booth, Ensign
Yose Fernand (from Argentina) and Captain
Yoshizo Soyeda (from Japan).

Members of the Young Women's Christian Association pose for C.W. Rutter in 1910. The Wisbech group
was based at the Alexandrina Club at 2 The Crescent.

The ladies of the YWCA about to embark on a summer bicycle excursion from Newton Rectory, 13 June 1917.

On several occasions Wisbech has celebrated royal events, such as Queen Victoria's coronation and jubilees, with a public dinner in the market-place. This marvellous photograph shows nearly two thousand people sitting down to a dinner supplied by Mr Bloodworth of the Red Lion Inn, North Brink, on Thursday 26 June 1902, in celebration of the coronation of King Edward VII. Unfortunately, owing to the king developing appendicitis, the actual coronation ceremony did not take place until Saturday 9 August.

Another view of the dinner in the market-place in celebration of Edward VII's coronation on 26 June 1902. After the dinner, around three-and-a-half thousand Wisbech schoolchildren were entertained to tea, courtesy of Mr John Baker of Colville House. Each child also received a coronation cup at Mr Baker's expense.

The civic procession passing along Bridge Street on the occasion of the funeral service for King Edward VII in 1910.

The proclamation of the accession of King George V in Wisbech market-place, on the afternoon of 11 May 1910. This postcard was published by Brown & Co.

King George V's accession is proclaimed for the first time from the Town Hall on Wednesday 11 May 1910. This postcard was also published by Brown & Co.

Wisbech Mart on the Old Market, 1920s. At this time the mart was of sufficient size to occupy Cornhill, Bridge Street and both market-places.

This Brown & Co. postcard shows the May Day celebrations in 1911, possibly on the Old Horse Fair.

The inhabitants of Sandyland celebrating May Day in 1908. The May Queen on this occasion was Florence Meynell. May Day festivities such as these continued well into the 1930s.

Wisbech St Peter's Scouts and Cubs on parade in St Augustine's Road during the Wisbech Scout Rally, 18 April 1928. Other participating troops included the Perse School, Cambridge, the Lynn (Wesleyan), the Leverington and the Cambridge University Rovers.

This picture from a lithographic slide produced by Brown & Co. shows a 'Robin Tea', held in the Public Hall, Hill Street; it was a Christmas party for the poorer children of Wisbech.

Members of the procession organized by the Social Committee of the NUR, photographed by H. Coates on 27 May 1923. The procession was one of a series of events including a concert in the Town Park by a massed band of around fifty players from the March railway and Wisbech town bands. Unfortunately the proceedings, which were held to raise funds for a town ambulance (and bath chair!), were cut short by a very heavy downpour.

This Brown & Co. postcard shows the crowd gathered outside the town hall to hear the declaration of the poll for the General Election on 26 January 1910.

A sombre gathering in Castle Square for the Remembrance Day Service in 1924.

This floral arch was constructed at the junction of Harecroft Road and Chapel Road to celebrate the granting of a peerage to Alexander Peckover in 1907. He was created Baron Peckover of Wisbech in recognition of his philanthropic acts within the county.

'This spree not quite so much row as when Mr Young came home. More class'; so comments the sender of this postcard, referring to the celebrations on the new Lord Peckover's return to Wisbech in 1907.

This procession, including firemen and pupils from the Barton School, is moving along Chapel Road past the Wisbech Arms. This postcard, by Leonard W. Smith of Lynn Road, may record another aspect of the town's celebrations for Lord Peckover's peerage in 1907.

Lady Asquith visits the Peckovers, 1914. Left to right: Lady Asquith, Lord Peckover, the Hon. Neil Primrose, and the Misses Peckover on the steps of Bank House (as Peckover House was then called). Lady Asquith later went on to open the 'Dickens Bazaar' held on 11 and 12 February 1914. This postcard was published by Brown & Co.

Lord Peckover opening the open air swimming baths built near the Swinging Berth partly as a memorial to the late Edward VII and partly to commemorate the accession of George V. The postcard was produced by Brown & Co. in 1912.

The opening of the bandstand in Wisbech Park on 9 July 1908, photographed by Vernon Bird of March. The bandstand was built by Wisbech Corporation 'at a cost not exceeding £100'. The minutes of the Corporation record the fact that Mr Wadsley, who rented the grazing rights in the park, offered no objection to the building of the bandstand although he did request a reduction in the rent – he received a rebate of £2 10s!

Wisbech dignitaries gather under canvas for the laying of the foundation stone for the extension to the North Cambridgeshire Hospital in 1914. The girls in the audience turning towards the camera are members of the choir of the Wisbech High School. This is another postcard produced by Brown & Co.

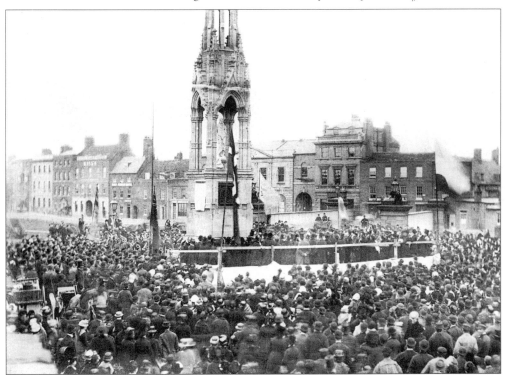

The unveiling of the Clarkson Memorial in November 1881. This monument was dedicated to Thomas Clarkson, Wisbech's greatest son, who was one of the leading campaigners for the abolition of slavery and the slave trade in the eighteenth and nineteenth centuries. The memorial was designed by Sir George Gilbert Scott RA, brother of the vicar of Wisbech, and cost £2,055, which was raised by public subscription.

Wisbech first received water pumped from Marham on 22 July 1865; however, it was not until 28 September that the great improvement was marked by a public holiday. This photograph by Edward Johnson shows the moment that the fire brigade pumped the water, via a hydrant in Castle Square, to a lamppost in the market-place which had been converted into a fountain. Unfortunately, the spray of water was carried by the wind and blew into the faces of the platform party!

The Rt Hon. David Lloyd George MP at Wisbech North station, 1920s. During this period Lloyd George travelled extensively throughout the Eastern Counties promoting the Liberal land policy.

Members of Wisbech fire brigade pose with a military detachment from the local Voluntary Aid Detachment Hospital for a postcard published by Brown & Co. during the First World War. Other organizations, such as the police force and Girl Guides, also provided brigades for the town ambulance.

Members of the Territorial Army on parade in the Crescent during the First World War. This is another postcard published by Brown & Co.

A large crowd gathered to witness the disbandment of the Cambridgeshire Home Guard in 1944. The ceremony was held on the playing field off Harecroft Road.

FROM FIRE
&
FLOOD . . .

Officers of the Wisbech fire brigade proudly standing in front of their recently acquired steam fire engine in the yard of the gas works. Purchased in 1885 the engine was christened Ettie *by Mrs Peating, Mayoress of Wisbech. The officers in the picture are, from left to right, Bugler Taylor, Conductor C. Gates, Superintendent Archer, Captain Plowright, First Engineer L.H. Palmer and Second Engineer F.G. Blott.*

Firemen damping down after Hutson's granary on West Parade was destroyed by fire, 16 October 1908. After the fire a potato warehouse was built on the site for R.E. Pratt. This was subsequently purchased by H.F. Mason.

Wisbech's horse-drawn steam fire engine pictured in attendance at a fire on West Parade *c.* 1900. The fireman in front of the engine is Henry O'Connor Palmer. The Palmer family had a long association with the Wisbech fire brigade.

This postcard, published in around 1910 by Brown & Co. of the Borough Studio, records one of the hazards facing motorists travelling in the Fens. Unfortunately, incidents like this one still frequently occur along the numerous drains and waterways in the district.

Frank Goldsmith Blott, Superintendent of the Wisbech Fire Brigade, resplendent in the uniform of the Horse Volunteers, c. 1880. Supt Blott served in the fire brigade for nearly fifty years, receiving a gold medal and a pension of £15 on his retirement in 1926.

The aftermath of a fire at Mr Whitehead's timber yard, South Brink Place, on 6/7 November 1884. The fire started in the evening and raged until the following morning. Initially the fire was fought using double lines of townspeople passing buckets of water from the river to the Wisbech engines. However, at midnight the steam fire engine from March arrived; able to draw water direct from the river using a suction hose, it proved more than a match for the fire.

A Denbighshire-registered car braves the highest tide for a hundred years on the North Brink, 2 March 1949. (*Courtesy of Elgood & Sons*)

AGRICULTURE

&

INDUSTRY

Landworkers laying straw between rows of strawberries in 1916.

Landworkers laying straw between rows of strawberries in 1916. Once a major fruit crop in the district, the strawberry industry has contracted considerably in recent times because of changing public tastes and influx of cheap imports from southern Europe.

Typical Fenland farm labourers take a break from making potato clamps, c. 1900.

A Cambridgeshire farm waggon of the early 1900s photographed by C.W. Rutter of Wisbech.

Buying and selling fruit produce on the Old Market, *c.* 1910. As a result of the hard landscaping and alterations to the layout of Old Market in the early 1990s, fruit and other crop auctions are now restricted to the Cattle Market.

Before the drainage of the Fens and the increase in agriculture, Fen people subsisted partly on eel fishing and wildfowling. This photograph of a wildfowler was taken by L.W. Smith in around 1912.

Trays of fruit produced by Arthur J. Quince, of Gadd's Lane, being taken to market along Chapel Road, *c.* 1900.

A chip basket factory in the 1920s. Firms such as English Brothers and British Basket & Besto Company produced thousands of chip baskets each year for the fruit industry. Wooden chips were gradually replaced by ones made of cardboard and nowadays plastic.

The interior of the roller house at Parson Drove woad mill in 1900. The three great rollers were used to crush woad leaves for dye. The process took about an hour and then the pulp was allowed to drain before being manually kneaded into balls. The mill was demolished just before the outbreak of the First World War in 1914.

A welcome break in the harvesting of woad plants at Parson Drove in 1900.

Mr Burnham with his horse, Tom, standing in the doorway of the roller house at Parson Drove in 1900. Three horses – one for each roller – were used to turn the great crushing wheels.

'Waddies' balling woad at Parson Drove in 1900. Once the woad leaves had been crushed, the pulp was kneaded and rolled by hand into balls approximately six inches in diameter. The large barrel was used to send the finished product to the dyers.

The drying ranges at Parson Drove woad mill in 1900. After the woad pulp had been kneaded into balls, the 'waddies' carried the balls – approximately twenty to a tray – to the drying ranges where it was left to dry for several weeks.

Joseph Oswin, bootmaker, of 1 Norwich Road, posing beside one of his stitching machines. This photograph was taken by C. W. Rutter in around 1920.

The interior of Gardiner's printing works, August 1919. The man on the left is Mr Staton, the machine minder, with his assistant, Albert Holman, with a Cossar printing press. The photograph was taken by the works foreman, A.J. Peggs.

The Chrysanthemum Show held in the Corn Exchange, North Brink, photographed by John Kennerell, c. 1890.

This First World War U-boat engine was recycled to generate electricity at Wisbech power station in Sandyland, from about 1920 to 1937/8. The engine was removed when Edmondsons changed the station

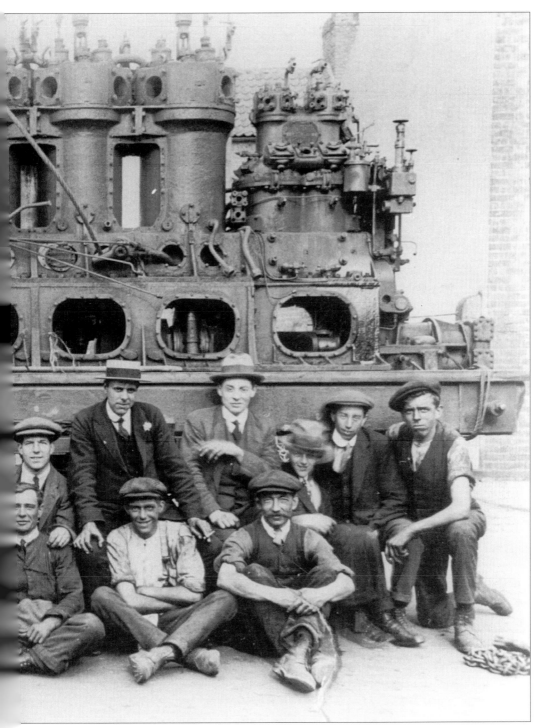

over from DC to AC. Among those in the group are H.B. Heath (manager), Alf Gillings (foreman) and
Ernest Merry (cable joiner). This postcard was produced by Alphonse Minten.

The workforce at Jas. Keiller & Son Ltd's jam factory at Wisbech, 1920s.

An advertisement for Elgood's beer. The Elgood family has run the brewery on the North Brink for over 120 years. Their involvement with the business originated in 1877 when John Elgood of Godmanchester and Peterborough (in partnership with George Harrison) bought the brewery from George F. Phillips. (*Courtesy of Elgood & Sons*)

A motorized dray outside Elgood's Brewery on the North Brink. The firm, which is one of the few small independent brewers in the region, has recently celebrated its bicentenary. To mark this event the old landscaped gardens near the brewery have been restored and the firm has introduced guided tours around the brewery. (*Courtesy of Elgood & Sons*)

A fine photograph of Nene Parade in the 1850s, possibly taken by Thomas Craddock. To the right is the Union Brewery which was owned at this time by Messrs Boucher & Jecks. The business was purchased in 1866 by George W. Mills of Downham Market and subsequently became known as Mills' Brewery. The establishment was owned by the Mills family until 1939 when it was sold to Messrs Hall, Cutlack and Harlock of Ely. Shortly afterwards brewing stopped and during the Second World War part of the building was used to house prisoners of war. The brewery was demolished to make way for the court house and police station which opened in 1957.

SECTION FIVE

SHOPS

W.V. Fundrey's staff and grocer's shop at 25 High Street, c. 1930. As well as offering goods 'All Made in Britain', Fundrey promised that his 'vans deliver in every part of Wisbech and District daily. A postcard will fetch us to your door.' How times have changed!

The Norfolk Street shop of Matthew Herrod, one time Mayor of Wisbech, photographed by C.W. Rutter, *c.* 1910. The business was later taken over by Philip Hudson and is now Ratcliffe's. One wonders how many modern pharmacists would be happy to sell both tobacco and medicine!

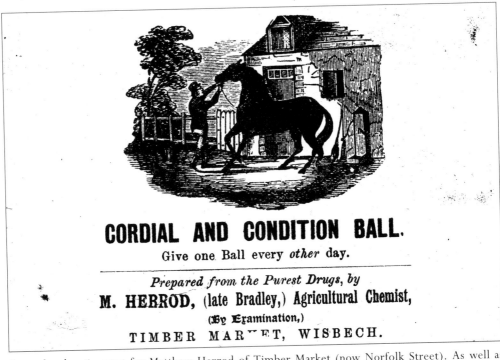

An early advertisement for Matthew Herrod of Timber Market (now Norfolk Street). As well as supplying medicines for both humans and animals, Herrod also designed and marketed agricultural machinery such as the Demon Sprayer, which was 'the Best Hand-Power Sprayer upon the Market. This sprayer has the largest sale in England'.

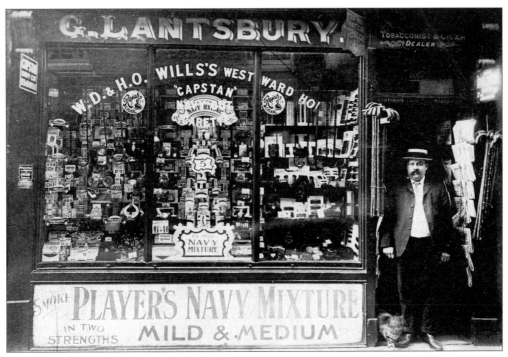

G. Lantsbury's tobacconist's shop at 103 Norfolk Street, *c.* 1910. By 1940 the business had been taken over by Orland Hunting & Co. Ltd, tobacconists.

Gardiner & Co.'s shop and offices at 10 Union Street, *c.* 1910. The windows are resplendent with all manner of patriotic souvenirs commemorating various events ranging from Queen Victoria's jubilee to the coronation of George V.

Gardiner & Co.'s premises at 11 Union Street. This half of the shop stocked stationery and artists' materials. This picture is one of a series of photographs taken by McNamara of Glasgow during February 1902.

Another view of Gardiner's shop and offices at 10 Union Street, February 1902. John Gardiner came to Wisbech from Leicester in 1836 to become the editor of the *Wisbech Gazette* which had been started to counteract the 'baneful influence' of the *Star in the East*. The latter was a radical newspaper supported by James Hill, the father of Octavia Hill, the famous social and housing reformer. By 1840 both the papers had folded. In 1845 Gardiner founded the *Wisbech Advertiser* which is now the *Citizen*. This is another picture from McNamara's series of photographs.

A magnificent display of root crops in the window of R.W. Green, seed and potato grower, 7 Cornhill, Wisbech. The swedes in the centre were grown by A. Cox Esq., no doubt from seeds bought from Mr Green!

EDUCATION, ARTS
&
SPORT

Th pupils and staff of Wisbech St Peter's Church Sunday School, photographed in September 1886.

Ladies engaged in an art class at the School of Art and Science (now the Angles Centre), *c.* 1900.

Keeping the ice clear for skaters on Virginia Waters, near Oldfield Lane, *c.* 1915. In the distance can be seen the signal and railway carriages on the line to Wisbech East station.

J. Sutcliffe Smith Mus. Bac. ARCO, conductor, pictured with members of the Wisbech Orchestral Society at Bowthorpe House, *c.* 1910.

Mrs Barret and her class at St Peter's School, *c.* 1905. The girls are wearing medals presented by the Isle of Ely Education Committee; each medal signifies one year's full attendance.

Gala Day at the Wisbech open air swimming baths, *c.* 1912. For this privilege the Swimming Club paid
the Corporation £1. Other charges at this time were swimmers 1*d*, spectators 1*d* and elementary schools
7*s* 6*d* per hundred children. The pool was reserved for ladies only from 11 a.m. to 2 p.m. on Thursdays.

Colville House *c.* 1885. The house was built by Thomas Steed Watson, three times Mayor of Wisbech,
and took its name from the fact that it was erected on land formerly owned by the Revd Dr Nathaniel
Colville. When the property passed to John Baker, who laid out Alexandra Road, he permitted cycle
races of national renown to be held in the grounds. An additional storey has since been added, and it is
now St Audrey's Convent.

Pupils and masters outside the original Grammar School in Hill Street, *c.* 1880. Thomas Clarkson, whose father John was headmaster at the time, was born here in 1760.

The second site of the Grammar School on South Brink, shown in this postcard view produced by R. Bennett in the 1920s. When the school in Hill Street was deemed inadequate to meet the pupils' needs, it was decided to relocate the school. A site was initially chosen off the Lynn Road but this was dropped when the premises of George Duppa Collins on the South Brink became available. After some alterations the school was opened here on 27 April 1897.

This postcard view published by Bennett Bros in around 1908 shows Wisbech High School viewed from across the Nene. The school was founded in November 1904 and was housed in Harecroft House which had been acquired by the Isle of Ely County Council after the death of Miss Susannah Peckover. In 1970 the school merged with Wisbech Grammar School forming a co-educational and comprehensive school based on the site. In the early 1980s the school became independent.

The Barton School was founded in the 1850s by Mr W.R. Stanton in a property formerly owned by Mr Jecks. Mr Stanton enlarged the original house and installed a heated swimming pool which was used throughout the year. After the school's closure the property was converted into an isolation hospital. Later on, it became a hotel before it fell into disrepair and was demolished in the 1980s.

Wisbech Working Men's Club and Institute, *c.* 1914. The top photograph shows the Institute Hall. Above the raised platform can be seen the portrait of Jonathan Peckover, the founder and first President of the Institute. The bottom photograph shows the reading room. At one time the Institute had more than a thousand members.

The officers of the Wisbech Working Men's Club and Institute, *c.* 1880. The Institute had many clubs and societies for football, draughts, chess, gymnastics, geology and the sciences as well as possessing a

substantial library. Two fundamental rules of the Institute were that it was strictly non-political and there could be no consumption of alcohol on the premises.

James Smart, Fenland ice skater. He was champion skater at ten miles and competed both in England and abroad. On 16 and 17 February 1887 he beat the noted Dutch skater, B. Kingma, at Slikkerveer, Holland. The photograph is taken from a *carte-de-visite* produced by John Kennerell at about this time.

George See was a member of another famous Fenland skating family. The half mile champion, See also raced at Slikkerveer, Holland, on 16 and 17 February 1887. He beat A. Van der Berg over 3,100 metres and over a mile on consecutive days. The times he achieved were then the fastest recorded. This picture is taken from another *carte-de-visite* produced by John Kennerell.

TRANSPORT

The Wisbech and Upwell tram on Elm Road, c. 1905. Opened in 1884, the passenger service was withdrawn in 1927 and closed completely in 1966.

The Wisbech to Upwell steam tram moving along Elm Road; this postcard was one of the 'Kingsway Real Photo Series' produced by W.H. Smith in the 1920s. This tram was the basis for 'Toby the Tram' in the Revd W. Awdrey's *Thomas the Tank Engine* children's books.

Workmen attempting to clean the Wisbech Canal, *c.* 1920. It needed scouring to remove silt that was deposited by the waters of the Nene; however, as the canal was used less and less, it was necessary to remove the rubbish that was thrown in by nearby residents.

Outwell Aquaduct, which carries the waters of the Well Creek over the Middle Level Main Drain, photographed by H. Coates & Sons in the 1930s.

J.H. Holmes's delivery van in Museum Square, *c.* 1910. Mr Holmes, a baker, traded from 19–20 Victoria Road.

Mr Joseph Oswin and passenger in an early dual-powered tricycle, photographed by A. Whiteman of 9 Norwich Road, at the turn of the century.

George E. Frisby's delivery cart, *c.* 1920. Mr Frisby's grocery shop was at 21 North Street; other members of the family had premises near the sluice.

Joseph Oswin of Norwich Road proudly posing, with a lady and her dog, on his motorcycle and sidecar for C.W. Rutter, *c.* 1910.

The aftermath of a fatal accident on a level-crossing near Wisbech in March 1910. Two men, Mr Tom Garner and Mr Alonzo Palmer, were killed when the motor car they were in was struck by an express train. The event received front-page coverage in the *Daily Mirror*. This photograph was taken by C.W. Rutter.

A busy day in the Midland Railway's goods yard, located to the north of Leverington Road, *c.* 1900.

The view from the platform of Wisbech East station looking towards the signal-box. (*Courtesy of Andrew Ingram*)

Wisbech East station signal-box controlled the main line and tramway movements within the station area – there were no signals on the actual tramway. The signalman would stand on the trackside platform to collect a tablet pouch from trains leaving the single-track Up main line. (*Information and photograph courtesy of Andrew Ingram*)

Wisbech East station, which opened in the spring of 1889, was the third station on (or near) this site. The East Anglian Railway used a temporary wooden structure from 1848 until it was replaced by the station of the Eastern Counties Railway which opened in 1855. (*Information and photograph courtesy of Andrew Ingram*)

Interior of Wisbech station signal-box, pictured in the 1960s. The Tyer's Apparatus by the window issued tablets for the signal-line section between Wisbech and Emneth. The 32-lever frame, shunting signal and point rodding were removed by volunteers from the North Norfolk Railway in 1969. (*Information and photograph courtesy of Andrew Ingram*)

Murrow was unusual in that it was a crossing point for branch lines of two separate railway companies – the London and North East Railway and the Midland and Great Northern Joint Railway. Each railway had its own station and signal-box. (*Courtesy of Andrew Ingram*)

A car breaker's yard, photographed by Alphonse Minten, *c.* 1920. One wonders what a modern Health &

Safety inspector would make of the improvised engine hoist!

A splendid view of sailing ships moored in Wisbech Port. Although this postcard was published by L.W. Smith of Lynn Road in around 1905, the absence of steam ships suggests that the original photograph may have been taken some thirty years earlier. In the 1850s as many as seventy ships are known to have been in the port at the same time.

This photograph of barges moored off the South Brink in the 1870s clearly shows the methods used to load and unload the barges that travelled either along the Nene to Peterborough and back, or via the Wisbech Canal to Outwell, Upwell and beyond.

The steam launch *Outwell Pride*, which took pleasure trips on the Nene, on the South Brink, *c.* 1910. The building to the left is the Octavia Hill Museum.

Richard Young's *Lady Alice Lambton*, with his newly built villa, Osborne House, in the background. This photograph was taken by Samuel Smith on 8 August 1853, the day before *Lady Alice Lambton* set off on an excursion to the Humber. Nearly a thousand people, including a band, were on board and many had come from as far away as Cambridge on special trains.

An orange boat unloading on the West Bank of the River Nene, *c.* 1950. The construction of Freedom Bridge in 1971 made views like these impossible.

Members of the Palmer family pose with their traction engine on Barton Lane, *c.* 1908. They are shown in the process of returning the dredger after it had undergone repairs.

The barquentine *Martinson* of Riga moored outside English Brothers' wood yard and photographed by Hardingham R. Mehew, 30 April 1898. For many centuries large quantities of timber were imported from the Baltic and Hanseatic ports via Wisbech.

Nene Parade, November 1894, photographed from West Parade as part of Poulton's Series. To the right is

the harbour line of the M&GN Railway which ran into the Old Market.

A fine photograph of a sailing ship moored off the West Bank, *c.* 1870. Ellis & Everard's 'Cake and Manure Stores' on the right has been demolished and is now the site of a car park. The large warehouse

next to this building is currently being converted into flats.

A horse-drawn milkfloat of Dickson & Hayes Ltd of Friday Bridge, 1960s. The days of the small independent dairies were already numbered.

THE VILLAGES

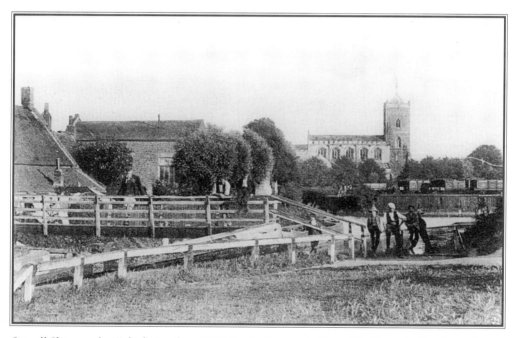

Outwell Sluice on the Wisbech Canal, c. 1905. In the distance, in front of St Clement's Church, can be seen wagons in Outwell tram depot.

The Tudor gatehouse to Beaupre Hall, Outwell, photographed by H. Coates & Son in the 1930s. The Manor of Beaupre Hall was a very ancient one, dating from the time of the Conquest. One of its more eccentric owners was Beaupre Bell, High Sheriff of Norfolk in 1706. At one time he kept over 500 wild horses, many of which were allowed to wander in and out of the Hall. After falling into disrepair the Hall was demolished in the 1960s.

Outwell Sluice on the Wisbech Canal, photographed by H. Coates in the 1920s. The building on the left is the sluicekeeper's cottage and the toll board is just visible.

The view looking west from the tower of St Clement's Church, Outwell, *c.* 1900. Outwell Sluice on the Wisbech Canal can be clearly seen and in the foreground to the left are the sidings of the Wisbech to Upwell Tramway which had recently been extended.

The view to the south from the tower of Outwell parish church, *c.* 1900. Outwell School can be seen just beyond the back yards of Church Terrace.

St Clement's Church, Outwell, photographed by H. Coates & Son in the late 1920s. A small group of people patiently wait for an omnibus on Norfolk Bridge.

This postcard of St Peter's Church, Upwell, was produced by C.W. Rutter, *c.* 1905. There have been three churches on this site, possibly more. The tower, including a spire, was built in the fourteenth century. Unfortunately, the spire became unsafe in the nineteenth century and was removed. However, there is a model of the church in the Wisbech & Fenland Museum complete with spire.

Racey's Mill, Emneth, photographed by H. Coates & Son in the early 1930s. The sails and cupola had been removed by this time and replaced by a warning light. In 1947 the tower was pulled down.

This photograph, reproduced from a postcard of C.W. Rutter, shows J.F. Racey's Wind and Steam Mills at Gaultree, Emneth, c. 1905. On the extreme right can be seen the Queen's Head public house.

The post office and T. Aitkins' bakery at Terrington St John, pictured on a postcard published by H. Coates & Son in the 1920s.

Terrington St John post office stores on the main road, another postcard view produced by H. Coates & Son, c. 1930.

Terrington St John's Church, photographed by H. Coates & Son in the 1930s. Although the parish lies in Norfolk, it belongs to the Diocese of Ely. Sandwiched between the tower and the main body of the church is what is called 'the Priest's House'.

The Volunteer Agricultural Camp at Terrington St John, photographed by H. Coates & Son in the 1930s.

Robert Bull, the sub-postmaster, outside Elm post office. After Mr Bull's death in 1926, the post office was run by his daughter Ellen. On her retirement the business passed to Mrs Eva Pooley (née Fox) who had lived with the Bull family since 1907. The business was divided in 1946 when the post office was transferred to Bridge House, J.R. Crown becoming sub-postmaster. Mrs Pooley retained the grocery shop until her retirement through ill health. On her death in 1978, her nephew left the contents of the shop, which included many of the original post office fittings, to the Wisbech & Fenland Museum, where they are still on display.

Elm High Road running alongside the Wisbech and Upwell Canal, as shown in a postcard published by H. Coates & Son in the 1920s. Across the canal to the left can be seen the substantial residence that was formerly Phillips Brewery, devastated by fire in 1911.

Halfpenny House in Halfpenny Lane, Elm, was built in about 1841 by Captain Read for one of his daughters. The name is believed to derive from the fact that the drainage rate for this area was a halfpenny per acre.

Handbell ringers posing outside All Saints' Church, Elm, photographed by F. Wright of Wisbech, *c.* 1880.

Canal Side, Elm, photographed from Elm Bridge by H. Coates & Son, *c.* 1920. Navigation along this part of the Wisbech Canal was discontinued in 1926.

The interior of All Saints' Church, Walsoken, photographed by H. Coates in the 1930s. To the left can be seen the fine font, highly decorated with perpendicular work, which was erected in 1544. The font's panels represent the Crucifixion and the Seven Sacraments – Baptism, Confirmation, Penance, the Eucharist, Holy Orders, Matrimony and Extreme Unction.

The interior of Wisbech St Mary's Church, photographed by H. Coates & Son, *c.* 1930. St Mary's was built towards the end of the fourteenth century. However, an earlier church, possibly Norman, may have existed on the site. Although the first vicar, the Revd Henry Jackson, was not appointed until the 1850s, it is believed that this parish may have been the mother parish of Wisbech St Peter's.

The village shop on High Road, Wisbech St Mary, photographed by H. Coates & Son, *c.* 1930. In 1929 the shop was run by John Greenwood Hanes.

6441 The Church, West Walton

St Mary's Church, West Walton, photographed by H. Coates & Son in the 1930s. The church's detached tower stands around 25 yards from the south side of the main building; one explanation for this is that, as it was built in a marshy country, any settling of the tower would have threatened the stability of the church.

The King of Hearts at West Walton, photographed by H. Coates & Son in the 1930s.

West End, Guyhirn, photographed by H. Coates & Son in the 1920s. The war memorial was dedicated by the Revd M.B. George on 25 July 1920. The cost of the memorial was around £200, which was raised by public subscription. In 1989 it was moved to the churchyard of St Mary Magdalene Church to make way for a new bridge on the A47 over the River Nene.

Moreton's Leam, Guyhirn, photographed by H. Coates, *c.* 1930. John Moreton, Bishop of Ely (later a cardinal), constructed the cut which straightened the course of the Nene in the fifteenth century.

Guyhirn Bridge, photographed by H. Coates & Son. The bridge was made of reinforced concrete and was opened for road traffic in 1925. It was replaced in 1992.

The iron bridge, known as Stephenson's Bridge, at Sutton Bridge which was opened on 24 September 1850. The bridge was sold twelve years later by the Cross Keys Bridge Company to the Peterborough, Wisbech & Sutton Bridge Railway for £12,500 cash plus railway shares.

The present Sutton Bridge, a swing bridge, was opened on 25 July 1897. It originally carried both rail and road traffic. This postcard view was published by H. Coates & Son in around 1930.

The watch hut and landing ground at No. 3 Armament Training Camp at Sutton Bridge, photographed by H. Coates & Son in the 1930s. Opened in the mid-1920s, the camp was used by the RAF as a base for bombing and gunnery practice. The aeroplanes are probably Hawker Furies.

The Peacock Inn, Sutton Bridge, before it was rebuilt. This pub was one of the many houses in the district tied to Elgood's Brewery of Wisbech. (*Courtesy of Elgood & Sons*)

The Peacock Inn, Sutton Bridge, after refurbishment. (*Courtesy of Elgood & Sons*)

The shop of E. Warrender, ironmonger, tinplate worker and general dealer, at Sutton Bridge, *c.* 1890. Next door is Philip White's butcher's shop.

A bill-sticker posing beside an example of his work outside the Oddfellows' Hall, Sutton Bridge, *c.* 1890. The Hall was later converted into a cinema.

The interior of Walpole St Peter's Church, looking west. This church, which is considered to be one of the finest in Marshland – if not in Norfolk - dates from about the year 1300. This photograph was taken by Edward Johnson and first appeared in *The Fen and Marshland Churches*, published by Leach & Son in the 1870s.

The unusual passageway underneath the high altar of Walpole St Peter's Church. This arched right of way was said to have been constructed owing to a dispute between the civil and church authorities. The founders of the church were refused permission to build *on* the road so they decided to arch it over with a roof. This photograph was taken by Daw of the High Street Studio, Hunstanton, at the turn of the century.

The Four Horseshoes public house at Throckenholt, Parson Drove, *c.* 1930. This pub is now a private residence. (*Courtesy of Elgood & Sons*)

The Red Hart, Three Holes, *c.* 1930. The hamlet of Three Holes derives its name from the bridge, constructed here in around 1610, which consisted of three arches each 8 feet broad. (*Courtesy of Elgood & Sons*)

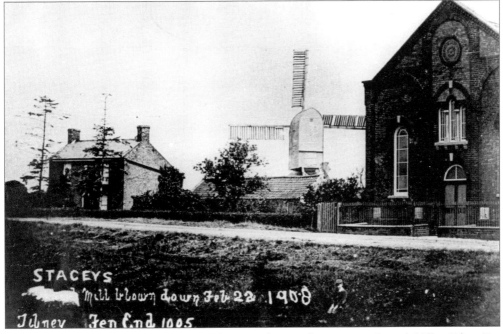

One of the many post windmills that studded East Anglia over the centuries, Stacey's Mill at Tilney Fen End came to a dramatic end during an electrical storm on Saturday 22 February 1908. During the storm a bolt of lightning struck the left-hand sail which fell and hit the fan-work; this prevented the mill turning into the wind and the building collapsed, killing the miller, Isaac Stacey, in the process.

Acknowledgements

The museum would like to thank the following people for the loan of photographs and for supplying additional information for the captions: Dr P. Cave, Mr P. Crofts, Mr & Mrs N. Elgood, Mr A. Ingram and Mrs B. Watson.

BRITAIN IN OLD PHOTOGRAPHS

To order any of these titles please telephone our distributor, Littlehampton Book Services on 01903 7215
For a catalogue of these and our other titles please ring Regina Schinner on 01453 731114